Early Intermediate

SEVEN MINOR MOODS

for Piano

by Glenda Austin

Seven Minor Moods is a collection of short pieces written in the white key minors.

I enjoy teaching minor pieces and always ask students to describe minor sounds. I'm never disappointed in their creativity and imagination. Some adjectives from them include: *melancholy, awkward, scary, sad, dramatic, anxious, creepy, mysterious, pensive, dark, gloomy,* and *cloudy,* to name a few.

When you play each piece, you'll clearly "hear" which adjective may match.

Teachers, I hope you will play this collection for your own easy listening pleasure.

Glenda Austin

ISBN 978-1-4950-1095-8

EXCLUSIVELY DISTRIBUTED BY

WILLIS MUSIC

HAL•LEONARD®

Visit Hal Leonard Online at
www.halleonard.com

Contact us:
Hal Leonard
7777 West Bluemound Road
Milwaukee, WI 53213
Email: info@halleonard.com

In Europe, contact:
Hal Leonard Europe Limited
42 Wigmore Street
Marylebone, London, W1U 2RN
Email: info@halleonardeurope.com

In Australia, contact:
Hal Leonard Australia Pty. Ltd.
4 Lentara Court
Cheltenham, Victoria, 3192 Australia
Email: info@halleonard.com.au

This collection was commissioned by the Joplin Piano Teachers Association (Joplin, Missouri)
to commemorate the 60th annual Marie Guengerich Piano Festival, 2016

Perilous Ascent

Glenda Austin

With rhythmic precision

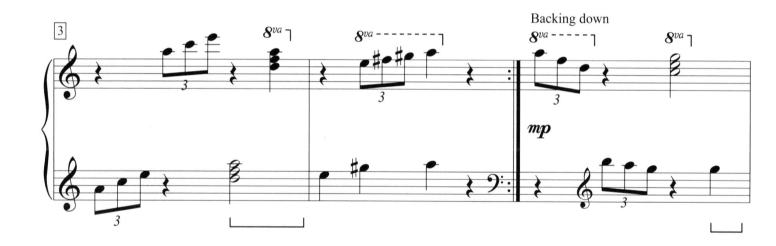

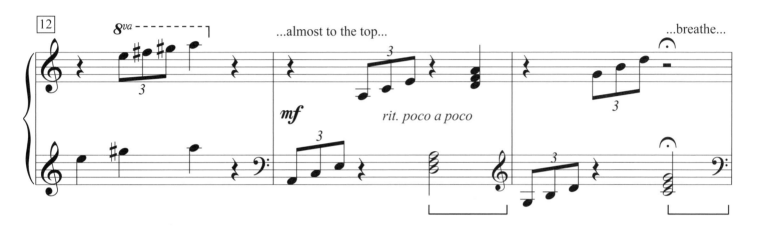

The Bungling Burglar

Glenda Austin

Mystical Maze

Glenda Austin

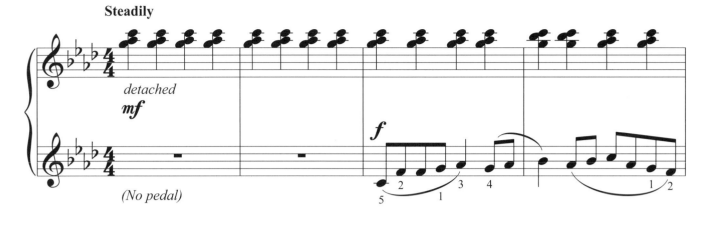

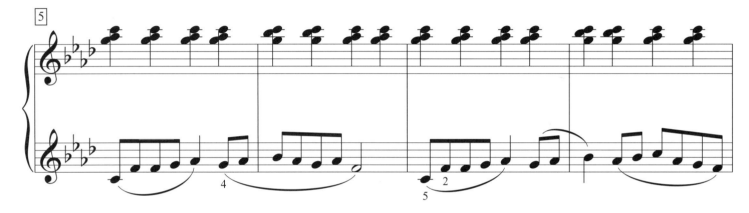

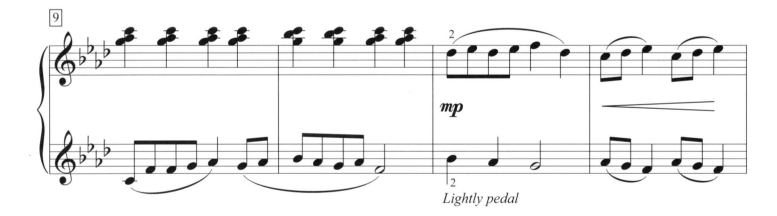

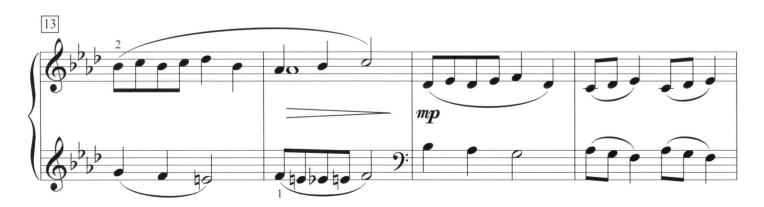

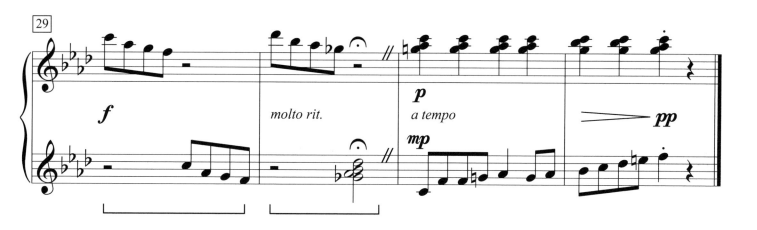

Adieu à l'automne

Glenda Austin

Midnight Escape

Glenda Austin

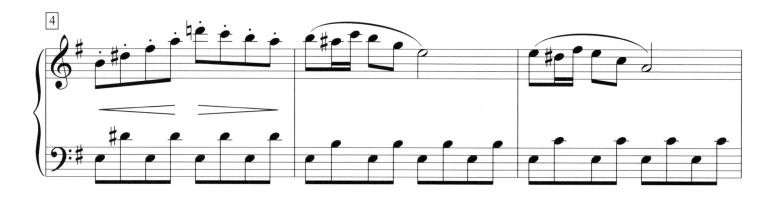

The Enchanted Moor

Glenda Austin

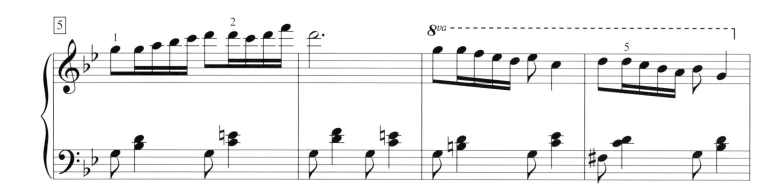

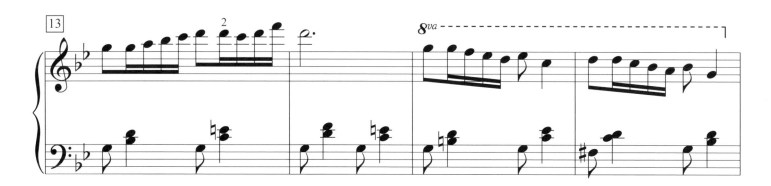

The Super Sleuth

Glenda Austin

Not too fast, with precision

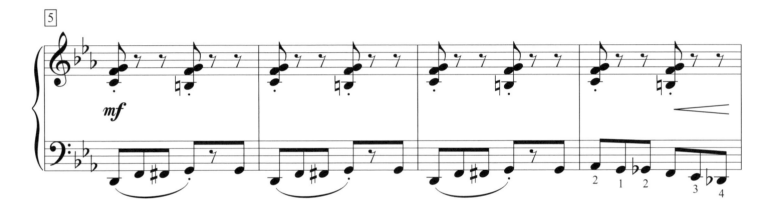

With light pedal

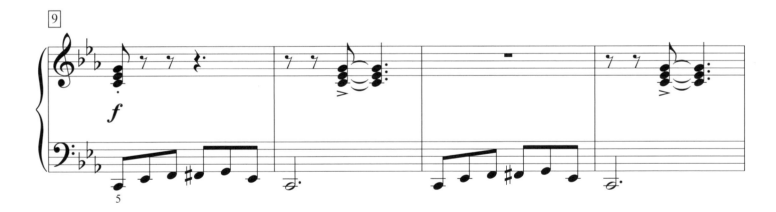

* a la "Perry Mason"

* A fictional defense attorney, based on books by Erle Stanley Gardner.
  "Perry" was later brought to life with a hit TV series from 1957–1966.